OPPOSITE

POEMS,
PHILOSOPHY
&
COFFEE

Opposite

Poems, Philosophy & Coffee

HELEN MORT &
AARON MESKIN

Valley Press

First published in 2019 by Valley Press
Woodend, The Crescent, Scarborough, YO11 2PW
www.valleypressuk.com

First edition, first printing (April 2019)

ISBN 978-1-912436-21-7
Cat. no. VP0141

A CIP record for this book is available from the British Library.

Cover photograph by Justin Slee.
Cover and text design by Jamie McGarry.

Printed and bound in the EU by Pulsio, Paris.

Contents

for Leeds

Introduction

HM: It's fitting that this collection of poems and responses starts with a piece called 'Testimony', set in Laynes Espresso in West Yorkshire because – like many good things – our project began with strong coffee. From 2014–2016, I was a Douglas Caster Cultural Fellow at the University of Leeds, a nebulous but exciting role which involved teaching, working on personal creative projects, supporting students interested in poetry and creating connections with other university departments. While based in the School of English, I worked on a number of structured projects, including a public art trail, a residency with the Law School and a project with the Alumni Office. But some of the most rewarding collaborations had a more informal genesis. Aaron and I started discussing connections between philosophical aesthetics and the aesthetics of poetry. Our conversations – which mostly took place in a cafe called Opposite – also turned to rap music, tattooing (and more coffee!) and I was particularly fascinated by Aaron's work on taste. Could a poem respond to some of the questions posed by a philosophical enquiry? I wasn't sure, but I wanted to find out.

AM: Like Helen, I was working at the University of Leeds when we met. I'm a philosopher of art or, if you like, an aesthetician. Aestheticians think about the philosophical issues raised by art, beauty and related matters: Can art be defined? What makes it valuable? Is beauty just in the eye of the beholder? They also think about specific art forms and distinctive aesthetic phenomena: I've worked on comic books, photography, video games, rap music, and the aesthetics and art of food. To be honest, poetry isn't a research focus of mine, even though I do have a longstanding interest in the form and occasionally teach material related to it in philosophy of literature classes.

But I admired Helen's poetry and we had some great conversations. It was exciting when she wrote a poem about a paper I had co-authored with my good friend, Jon Robson. And this suggested a possibility that really interested me — a non-standard form of collaboration between an artist and a philosopher (or, as it turns out, a group of philosophers). I had just finished a project where I read philosophy with, and danced alongside, four local dance improvisers. Maybe the project with Helen wouldn't be quite as weird as that, but it promised to be interesting and enjoyable.

HM: I was excited and inspired by the papers Aaron had begun to send to me, particularly Eva Dadlez's work on the status of tattoos as works of art. As I began to try to write poems in response, I sometimes got a little weighed down by the idea of trying to make my creative responses 'hold' or contain some of the theory explored so eloquently in the papers. In short, I was trying to make them too directly philosophical. The resulting pieces were abstract and seemed dead on the page. When I returned to Eva's paper for another read, I decided to try a different approach and react to her consideration of tattooing-as-art by creating my own version of a portrait, a sketch (in words) of famous tattooed lady Betty Broadbent. This response was much more tangential than the pieces I'd tried previously and freed me up to react to the theories and proposals I was encountering in a looser way. I couldn't hope to paraphrase the philosophers I'd been reading, nor should I try. This needed to be a dialogue, a sprawling conversation, the kind you might have in a bar late at night.

AM: There are all sorts of interesting issues lurking around here about the relationship between poetry and philosophy. Philosophers have explored abstractness in poetry and its relation to the abstractness of philosophy.[a] The question of whether – and how – poems and other literary works can be philosophical is a recurring one.[b] And aestheticians have disputed with one another about poetry and paraphrasability; that is, whether the meaning of a poem (if it has meaning!) can be put into other words.[c] The experience Helen describes above raises a related question: Can works of philosophy be paraphrased poetically? And, if so, would there be any value to doing this?

I meant what I said about lurking. The questions I've mentioned are not fully out in the open here. That is, they are not explicitly addressed within this book. Helen's poems don't seek to confirm or disconfirm any specific hypotheses about poetic meaning, the poetry-philosophy relationship, or the nature of poetic abstractness. Nor did she end up responding to any philosophical works that are specifically about poetry. But that those issues are not fully out in the open does not mean they are not present in some sense.

Here's another question that is present – one that hasn't been addressed as often in the philosophical literature. Philosophy is usually evaluated cognitively and epistemically. A successful work of philosophy solves problems, provides insights, produces knowledge, inculcates wisdom. But what about philosophy's role in inspiring art? Does a philosophical work's capacity to stimulate creativity count as a philosophical virtue? Or is that just a valuable side-effect?

HM: What you'll find inside the pages that follow is not an exhaustive attempt to answer the questions that a collaboration between a poet and aestheticians might raise. As a writer, I don't always trust definitive answers. Like the narrator in Walt Whitman's 'Song of Myself', I believe that we contain multitudes (as researchers and as humans) and that we contradict ourselves often. I've always been drawn to poetry's strange mix of provisionality and rhetorical authority, the way even a simple sonnet can embody a paradox. So this collection is not a set of propositions or conclusions. Instead, it's a record of a fascinating series of conversations: between people, between poems and papers. Each of the poems here was written in response to an article. And in each case the author or authors of the paper have responded to the poem. We hope that these dialogues capture some of the exhilaration you feel when you encounter new ideas for the first time, talk to a person whose skills and understanding are different from yours. In short, we hope they capture some of the spirit of our conversations in Opposite Cafe. We've provided the poems and the philosophy, you just need to make your own coffee.

AM: While you make yourself a cup – perhaps just in your imagination – I thought I should tell you a bit about how we selected the articles and approached the contributing philosophers. We did not do things in an especially systematic way! Rather, I chose articles (all in philosophical aesthetics and published in the last ten years or so) that I found engaging, that weren't especially 'lost in the weeds', that connected with Helen's interests, and that were written by people who might be excited by the project. And for the most part this not-so-methodical approach worked – Helen found something interesting to say in response to almost everything she read, and every one of the philosophers we approached about the project was willing to participate.

We didn't give much guidance to the philosophers. I asked them to write a response in about 500 words and told them the format was open. They were given the opportunity to contact Helen if they wanted to ask her about the poem, but most of them wrote their responses without contacting her. We hope you find those responses as interesting as we do.

Bibliographical information about the articles that inspired Helen is provided in the back of the book.

HM and AM: This book is dedicated to Leeds. It's where we worked when we met. It's where we drank coffee and planned the project. Aaron lived there for more than thirteen years. It's a great city. But there is a lot of inequality in Leeds, and there are many people there who need assistance. For that reason we've decided to donate our royalties to a Leeds charity which is working to improve things in the city. So 50p from each copy of the book sold will be donated to the Leeds Community Foundation's Healthy Holidays campaign which enables vulnerable children in Leeds to have access to food and fun activities during the school holidays. For more information about LCF, see www.leedscf.org.uk.

POEMS &
RESPONSES

Testimony

My coffee cooling in a tiny, frosted glass.
I don't have to taste it to know it's good.
I sit beneath a triptych of pale photographs:
a sea no one can swim in, an Oslo wood,

dense branches lit so sharply they could cut.
The woman opposite dissects her almond cake.
Sweetness is dissolving on my tongue, abrupt,
then lingering. I don't have to see your face

to see you. The water rises past the frame.
The forest unpeels from the canvas, steps clear.
I don't need to say your name
or ever think of you to keep you near.

— HM

Testimony, Acquaintance, Coffee, Poetry

Do you need to drink the coffee in order to know how it tastes? Many philosophers have said yes, first-person experience of the coffee, as with any item of food or drink, is required in order to know what it tastes like. In fact, they have argued that this feature of our gustatory judgments is something that links them to our critical judgments about art. To know whether an artwork is beautiful or otherwise aesthetically valuable, they argue, requires first-person experience of that artwork. So gustatory judgments are, at least along this dimension, akin to critical judgments.

In our essay, 'Taste and Acquaintance', we argue that this philosophical view is mistaken.[d] There are many ways in which one can come to know what a coffee tastes like without tasting it yourself, most notably via the testimony of others. And we have argued, in other places, that something similar is true about critical judgments.[e] Much of what we know, we know because others have told us. This is true about food and art, just as it is about science and history (although this is not to deny that there are also important differences between these cases).

The poet, or more precisely the poetic narrator, agrees with us. She doesn't need to taste the coffee to know it's good. In this case, we suspect the narrator has had many prior delicious coffees at the place where her coffee cools. If so, the basis for her knowledge of the coffee is induction. All prior coffees here have been delicious. Therefore, this coffee will be delicious. Not a perfect source of knowledge, but good enough in most cases.

What happens next? Not an argument.

The poetic narrator describes a photograph. Photographs are another way one can know what something is like without experiencing it directly. In this respect they seem to be akin to testimony (though, of course, in other respects they are importantly different).

The narrator can know what the Oslo wood is like, or at least some of what it is like, without being there. And there is a sea (a thing seen?) no one can swim in – another thing the photograph provides access to which is not directly experienced.

Of course, it can sometimes seem as if the photographed object is, in some sense, really there. The forest, the sea, whatever is depicted in the photograph 'steps clear'. Or, at least, seem to do so.

The poem is addressed to someone – someone partially hidden or gone. (Is it possible to see someone without seeing their face? Not hard if you see the rest of them!) What about keeping someone near without saying their name or ever thinking of them? We can imagine a number of ways in which one might do this, but what's interesting to us is the fact that the poem ends with this ambiguous claim. The indeterminacy seems important.

Could you know what this poem is like without experiencing it yourself? Could you know what it is like to experience its ending? Would testimony be enough? Suppose someone tells you it's a good poem but you haven't read it? What about induction?

We believe that one could know a great deal about the poem in such circumstances. But something would surely be missing. What is it?

— JR and AM

Bad Art

Don't tell me I can't love the Monet-blue
of a VK bottle in Livingstones nightclub
as a girl who might have bullied me at school
lifts it to her mouth and prints the rim
with *Hot Flamingo* pink. Don't tell me I can't
love the evening light reflected in the sheen
of a Red Bull can, crushed and sculptural
in a bouncer's hand. All this was fifteen years ago
and I'm watching from the future, its tasteful
duck-egg and wool-carpet corridors,
its cavernous halls which give exactly the right
acoustic for a Mahler symphony, its
French subtitles, its novelistic urban view;

the sympathetically-translated future,
the place I live in, always squinting
back at the sticky cloakroom desk where I
wrote bad poems on the backs of till receipts
and smoothed my cheap haircut, tapped
my white stiletto heels to the rhythm
of the *Cha-cha Slide* and peered at the dancefloor
saw a man in a *World Pole Vault Championships*
t-shirt and caterpillar moustache jump and wiggle
out of time, the way he'd pause at the slow songs,
sway with someone held invisible between his arms,
against his chest, how predictable it all was then,
how perfect.

— HM

19

Magic Grace in Tragic Taste

Some art is *so bad that it's good*: movies like *The Room*, bad paintings at the Museum of Bad Art, bad novels by Harry Stephen Keel. This stuff – call it good-bad art – is puzzling. How could anyone ever love this stuff? How could something be good *because* it's bad? In a paper we wrote, Matt Johnson and I tried to address this puzzle.[f]

According to our view, these works are artistic failures; the artists did not succeed. That's why these works are bad. But the artist's failure generates a kind of bizarreness. The original intention deviates so far from the finished product, and we're left bewildered: *How could anyone think this is a good idea?* This bewilderment or bizarreness is what makes these works good.

Usually art is good when its aesthetic value is a result of artistic success. We ordinarily like art because it's made well. But this doesn't happen in good-bad art. In good-bad art, the failure – the badness – makes it bizarre, and that bizarreness is what makes it good.

Some folks say that we like bad art because we take pleasure in the artist's massive failures. If this view was right, enjoying good-bad art would be a kind of schadenfreude; your enjoyment of *The Room* would be morally questionable. In our view, it's not. You don't enjoy the failure; you appreciate the unintended bizarreness that results from the failure.

The poem reminds us that bad art is all around us. We write bad poems, we listen to bad music while doing bad dances. Bad art is even more common if we're generous in what we think of as art – if we think of ourselves making little flashes of art out of our ordinary lives. It's not just our music and our poems that are bad.

Bad art is also in our haircuts and moustaches, our wrestling t-shirts, and our white stiletto heels. And we love it.

At least, we love it later. The poem brings out a connection to the past. We laugh at our youthful sensibilities: *Can you believe I listened to Switchfoot? Can you believe I wore those colours?* But deep down, we love them. The bad art and style of our youth is a yearning for the past – 'how predictable it all was then, / how perfect' – perfectly and predictably shitty. The colours were gaudy, but the gaudiness only makes them better. The gaudiness makes the past stick out – it contrasts against the present, perpetually cool and steely and contemporary. Maybe that's what makes our past styles perfect in their predictability; their reliable shittiness shields us, providing comfort from the changing present.

This speaks to the view that Matt and I have. The bad style of our past selves is good because it's bizarre, not because it's a massive failure. Often, the perfect shittiness of a past style makes it seem foreign and strange: *Was that really me?* We're not mocking our past selves. There's no schadenfreude here, just bewilderment.

There's also a difference. Our claim is that good-bad *art* is bizarre because of failure. But the bizarreness of good-bad *style* doesn't require any failure at all. Just the opposite; you rocked that 90's look perfectly. That's what makes it so deliciously tragic.

— JD

The Angler

'Climbing is something like dance'
– Thi Nguyen

and since I don't dance these days
the movement stays bunched
in my calves and fingertips,
knotted in my shoulderblades

or I hold my hand out to the slab
and find it shimmying away from me,
asked by someone else. The daylight moon
is a backwards glance. The grass shivers

with laughter. Granite moves
with a new partner. I admire him:
bouldering above a river, and
the river rising through him

until their dance is tidal,
his body lapping at the sky
and never changing it
the ground drawing him back.

— HM

The Rock is the Dance Teacher

I spent the first thirty years of life essentially immobile, by my own choice. I was a sitter, a reader, a thinker. It was not so much that I despised my body as that I was profoundly detached from it. It didn't respond well to my commands; it was a distant and clumsy attachment to my true mental self. So I ignored it, and spent my time doing the things that avoided its use.

Eventually, bodily disuse lead to constant pain, and I ended up on a long path that started in yoga and ended up in a deep love of rock climbing. This was something of a shock. I never expected to become the kind of person who craved a physical activity. I never expected that I would start savouring the intensity, the absorption, and even the physical pain of climbing.

It was only years later, when I starting writing about games and game aesthetics, that I put together why, after a life of being repulsed by exercise, I fell for climbing. Rock climbing presents an endless series of new and fascinating little logic puzzles to solve with your balance, your strength, and your finesse. Climbing is a game, played in the language of movement.

The movements that climbing called out of me became rapturous. I'll sit back, days after a climb, and savour the memory of all that sensuous, lovely motion – how I put this foot balanced just so, how I inched myself desperately over, just barely in balance. Climbing is thrilling; it is difficult. And it is beautiful precisely because it is thrilling and difficult. Climbing movements are elegant, not just as abstract movements, but as solutions to problems.

The way I put it in my article, 'The aesthetics of rock climbing', is that climbing cultivates a self-reflective aesthetic.[g] We appreciate the aesthetics of our own movement – its grace, its elegance, its loveliness.

Helen Mort's poetic response begins with a narrator explaining why they do not climb. 'I don't dance these days,' they say. 'The movement stays bunched in my calves and fingertips, / knotted in my shoulder blades.' This sounds, to me, exactly like how I felt before I started climbing. My movement was bunched and pooled. But it was climbing that integrated me – it somehow put me in touch with my body, made it not a distant thing, but something I immediately inhabited. Before climbing, my hands were the only part that felt like me. I used them to type, to cook, to do origami. The rest of my body was a swamp, through which the movement filtered sludgily. Climbing got that sludge fast-flowing.

Interestingly, the reason I think that climbing was so successful at integrating me is precisely because it is a game, and not just a free form dance. The rock forces moves out of you. Often, there is only one movement pattern for you that will get you through. And the rock forces you to learn it, by threatening you with swift and brutal punishment. In yoga, you can cheat, and unless the instructor is watching you, you can get away with it. The rock does not forgive. Be sloppy, and the rock spits you off.

That unforgiving, binary nature helped me figure out how to move with subtlety and care. I had a clear target and immediate feedback. The rock forces you to become sensitive to your body. You don't have to know how to dance to start climbing. The rock is your teacher, and your guide.

— CTN

Itch

geranium-scented
    badly-lit
I stand at the bathroom window
    watched
by a silver eucalyptus
scratching   the full-moon
roundness of my belly
where skin   is clay
    cast in a new mold
cast over
    your limbs your spine
    persistent heart
where   this prickling
    this crawling
this delicious   ache
might be your breath   passing
    through me
your own itch
to run   into this world
feet first   and fierce
    unscratchable

— HM

Knowing Together

I

The mother scratches her taut belly, and on the other side of that scratched skin is a being who feels the touch and may touch back, kicking, stretching, hiccupping.

Who said that somatic experience is private? Producing sensations in each other through entanglement of our bodies is surely one of the purest forms of communication, just as it is one of the purest manifestations of beauty. (Yes, beauty: why would beauty be detached, hypothetical?)[h]

My body knows you: it reads the state of your soul off the feeling of your shoulders tensely perched under my hands. It reads the contours of your needs and wants as the needle reads a vinyl record.

My body knows myself with you. My spasming stomach knows the anger my mind has yet to grapple with. Or, on a better day, I know my desire for you through the sensation that every cell is standing on end, straining for space on a surface soon to be touched.

A pressure you apply to my body can comfort, caution, relieve pain, convey understanding. The sensation of our bodies together heals me: your arms weighing on me, the movement of our breathing together, the warmth of your skin that I know as warmth on my lips, our pulse (whose?). The sensation is a knowing of what our bodies are creating, transmitting, receiving: call it, for simplicity, love.

2

The mother feels an ache, accented by geranium and eucalyptus, that will not be absorbed into the pat narrative of pregnancy as a litany of pain and heaviness and nausea and exhaustion. She feels into it, its crawl, its prickle, and feels outward from it, tracing what may be a signal to its source.

The freshness of the sensation snaps the moment into shape, calls the mother to attention, prompts inquiry. This delicious ache is to be savoured and also investigated, a point of contact with a being that is building itself out of her very body.

Is my ache your breath? Your itch? What can I know of you through your body cradled within mine? What can you know of me as you float there, pressed among my organs, feeling my muffled scratch on your spine? We feel our way to each other, recognize each other as sturdy masses and shifting pressures, each of us perpetually reshaped by the other.

This moment of sensation, this felt beauty, is the beginning of knowledge that demands to be multiplied. Through my body I find myself, and you.

— SI

Street Art

for Daryl

You turned your son's name
into a breathing dragon, red and tangerine

and you turned the Cornbrook
tramline vista into fire,

made a man on the platform turn
into a statue, rapt in scrutiny,

the moors behind him
burning with the day's last heat.

The outline done,
you turned on your heel,

turned with the assurance
of a boy doing wheelies

on a street in Hulme,
landing every one just right, turned

back into yourself
head-down on Oxford Street

and the shadows from the bridges
wrote across you as you walked

and the city was your spray-can,
shaken, ready to be lifted.

— HM

The Art of Turning

Graffiti writers literally write themselves into existence: find a name, ease into a style, and put it up everywhere. The process can take you from having nothing to being something with little more than a fat-tip marker or a Krylon can. But the graffiti artist transforms by transfiguring – an alley wall, a city mailbox, a subway car. The poem 'Street Art' highlights this mutual transformation – mutual transfiguration – through which graffiti empowers its practitioners and illuminates the cityscape.[i]

As we read the poem we seem to watch the graffiti artist from a distance – a spatial distance but also a hint of temporal distance. We watch the artist confidently make an outline and venture off into the city. And we hear admiration in the narrator's voice, but we cannot discern its source – is this a lover's admiration? A friend's? A sibling's? Whatever its source, there's intimacy here, history, time. There is something concrete, city-like, between them. What the narrator seems to see is not just someone writing themselves into existence, but someone rising from some vague darker place, farther back – shadows from the bridges – into a new life.

The poem opens with familiar themes from pop graffiti: dragons, fire, magic, Medusa (turning to stone). These images have a striking dual purpose; they illuminate the mind with the colour and imagery of graffiti and key us into a poem about turning: transformation, renewal, transfiguration. 'You turned your son's name / Into a breathing dragon.' These pop-graffiti images are also images from Greek mythology: dragons, fire, rapture, burning – we think of the phoenix, the great symbol of renewal, rising from the ashes. As the artist writes graffiti, they turn into themselves. The moors, the uncultivated lands, are behind them. The artist is cultivating, becoming someone.

These images of renewal and the repetition of the word 'turn' prepare us for the central move in the poem, which, aptly, comes right in the middle:

> The outline done,
> you turned on your heel,
>
> turned with the assurance
> of a boy doing wheelies

To 'turn on your heel' is idiomatic for departing rapidly or suddenly turning away from something. Once you've popped a wheelie it's not so easy to turn back – best done with assurance. The outline must be solid, definitive. Having been prepared with images from Greek mythology, 'turned on your heel' also evokes Achilles' heel and, through the boy's wheelies, juxtaposes the poem's focus on renewal with play – two concepts that are central to the aesthetics of graffiti. In this way the poem playfully flips or turns the concept of Achilles' heel: whatever darkness is there in the artist's past is now being leveraged to make something out of nothing, to turn on their heel and rise from the ashes with nothing more than a spray can. In other words, Achilles' heel – a weakness in spite of overall strength – becomes a strength in spite of weakness. Making something from next to nothing.

And now those shadows land in a different light. They write across the artist as the artist just wrote across the city. Lifting them up now. The city is shaken, the artist assured. Both lifting, changed, ready to be lifted.

— NR

Christina at the Super Bowl

She's turning the word *brave* into a highway with no speed limit
where SUVs with bullbars juggernaut towards the light,
their tiny drivers whooping behind sunglasses. She's breaking

the raised glass of night. She's levitating in her diamond stilettos.
Her voice is coffee with eight sugars, a waffle-stack
the size of Canada. Her mouth is a bowler's empty hand

after the throw but the players bow their heads
and lower their shoulders anyway, a man with cornrows
bites his trembling lip, sways to the pitch of her vibrato

and I feel the lurch I felt in English class at primary school
when I read my story out too loud under my breath
and Miss Long darted from her wooden stool

to snatch my book away and hiss *pipe down.*
No one likes a show-off Helen. Afterwards,
I ran hard from her pleated skirt and pleated frown

ran to the field's edge and shouted til my voice was gone,
yelled from the hill where we once rolled painted Easter eggs,
a contest where the brightest, gaudiest one won.

— HM

Less is More?

'Christina at the Super Bowl' captures the ambivalence I felt and still do feel around thinking and writing about excess in art and performance.

When I was writing my article and thinking about Aguilera's performance, a snatch of a different poem kept running through my head.[j] I kept coming back to the lines in Marianne Moore's poem 'Silence' that go: 'The deepest feeling always shows itself in silence; not in silence, but restraint.' I have always loved that poem and those lines in particular. The idea that strong feelings, indeed the strongest feelings, can also be the quietest and most contained, seems to capture an important truth.

Silence deserves our respect. It is too often seen as a retreat, as a sign that someone doesn't have the right words, or doesn't know how to respond. Yet so often the opposite is true. We are afraid of silence and of sitting still. We fill up silence with words, any words, because we lack patience to wait for the right words. Or we don't have the wherewithal simply to hold the space for another person and be silent with them.

Not coincidentally, the art I most admire and feel most drawn towards is restrained, economical, and for want of a better word, 'tasteful'. Most of the time I'll take Ella Fitzgerald's careful pauses over almost anyone's vocal pyrotechnics, a jazz trio over a 40-piece band, and a still life of two peaches over a crowded canvas.

At the same time, I understand that the line about silence and restraint in Moore's poem is not without irony. The speaker of the line is Moore's father, whom she gently sends up. I understand that silence can be evasive and even cruel. And I understand that what is tasteful can be boring.

More importantly, I understand that ideals of restraint and good taste have been used to keep women and minorities down. Calls for 'civility' are used to put down those who are trying to rectify injustice. And words like 'gaudy' and 'show-off' can contain judgments that go far beyond aesthetics. In Helen Mort's poem, the teacher who remonstrates with the narrator is not just imparting a lesson about reading. She's imparting a lesson about how her young, female charge should be in the world: quiet, unassuming, and not an imposition on others.

And so, as much as my article is an attempt to understand what 'good taste' and 'excess' mean for musical performance, I admit to reservations about the project. Even if I won't join Mort in running to the field's edge and yelling my lungs out, I'm grateful that there are people who do.

— JB

Chalet Lines

Wine-stained and gig-drunk, we pitched our bodies home and I
    asked you
to play me something beautiful, something beyond the cavern
of your kitchen, the moonlit garden's slant, your mouth, your hands
on the tabletop, the foxes calling desperately outside, as if those things

were not enough. You chose Belle and Sebastian, a flickering song
in black and white called 'Chalet Lines'. You tapped your feet in time.
I closed my eyes and saw the boys from the amusement park, the
    shadow-
carousel, the smear of his reflection on the window afterwards

and when I pushed my glass aside and turned away from you,
it wasn't because I'd heard a man's voice savouring that melody,
it wasn't the easiness of rhyme, the neatness of the words
I had just said no for the final time, or the pregnancy test ad

that YouTube flashed up afterwards, it wasn't hearing
human voices in the foxes' cries. It was the word *raped*,
how they had made it glassy, elegant. How it rolled like a marble
through the song, entered the room and how you let me pocket it.

— HM

Art and Sexual Assault

I would like to begin by thanking Helen very much for turning her attention to my work.[k] I consider her poem a beautiful gift that I shall treasure. I am also grateful to Aaron for making this unique volume happen.

When I started studying art history as an undergrad, I was struck by how many important paintings in the European canon in some way or another eroticised sexual assault. Many of these were taken from Greek and Roman mythology, especially mythological poetry: Danaë, Persephone, Leda, Europa, Io, and the other victims of the so-called 'loves of the gods'. A related noteworthy topic is the mythological history involving the rape of the Sabines. Some of the greatest masters of the European tradition made such paintings: Titian, Michelangelo, Poussin, Picasso. Some fine poets also found inspiration in this topic: e.g. Shakespeare writing about Lucretia, and Yeats about Leda.

Once I started thinking about these paintings and poems as works dealing with rape, rather than seduction or something similarly romantic, two things become salient. First, all of these works portray or describe rape in a way that makes it sexy and appealing. Second, they all suggest or imply that the rape in question yields some benefit for the victim. This is important because these are also two features of what has come to be called 'rape culture', where rape is not just pervasive but also normalised and trivialised and victims are blamed. Of course lots of cultural forms participate in rape culture, but my worry about the paintings and poems I just mentioned is that they are especially adept at making rape beautiful, sexy, and appealing.[l]

I am glad to be invited to think about 'Chalet Lines' in this context. On the one hand, this song does not at all belong in the tradition of works briefly discussed above. Sung by a man, the perspective is one of sympathy with the victim and poignantly expresses her hopelessness and misery – at least this is how the song is commonly interpreted, and I see no reason to disagree. The audience is in no way invited to take voyeuristic erotic delight in rape (unlike the works mentioned above, the focus is on the aftermath rather than the act itself), nor to blame the victim or imagine that she somehow benefited from rape. It's clear, I think, that this song aims to foreground and make us feel at least a little of the anguish that rape causes.

On the other hand, as Helen beautifully highlights, Stuart Murdoch sings a simple melody with such sweetness that it almost sounds like a lullaby (my word, not Helen's). I like the way Helen puts it: Murdoch 'savours' the melody. While never cloying, Murdoch's voice is undeniably soothing, even if a bit sad. The result is that the word 'rape' is made, as Helen astutely observes, 'glassy' and 'elegant' and rolls 'like a marble through the song'. You could almost find yourself humming while doing household chores, 'He raped me in the chalet lines…' Almost.

I take it that one point of the song is precisely this stark contrast between the violence and violation that 'rape' is meant to conjure, and that the song emphasises in taking the victim's perspective, and the tranquility and sweetness that the melody and Murdoch's voice conjure. So unlike, say, Titian's handling of rape, this song is utterly self-aware that it is dealing with rape in a way that, at least on one hand, lulls and pleases. I think 'Chalet Lines' is a song that is supposed to disturb in just the way that Helen highlights. If you're tapping your toes and humming along blithely to a beautiful melody, you're basically missing the whole song.

— AWE

Oil on Canvas

My mind is a bad sitter. It is pictured
in motion – half in the red armchair,
half out of it. My mind wears
an expensive dress and cheap shoes.
It refuses a wristwatch. In the background,
there's a black greyhound, a fireplace,
the shape of someone else's mind
as it gently closes the door
or tidies away the blue-patterned mugs.

My mind has finished all the wine.
My mind wants to hide its bitten fingernails.
My mind is singing a 1990s pop song
but you can't tell. My mind has never seen
your mind before, and now
its hair is the wire
behind a light switch,
its cheeks are rhubarb,
its eyes follow you
all the way round the room.

— HM

Turning the Picture On

The poet's mind is a tease. It dances out of reach, reluctant to be pinned down. It's full of contradictions. It's not at all isolated, but connected in many ways – to a warm living space, a black dog, blue mugs, another person. It's constituted by thoughts and memories, habits and tastes. Helen Mort seems to be saying that she, and maybe others as well, are too evanescent for a portrait painter to depict.

I would respond by saying: That's precisely the marvel of portraits! This poet is an artist, with special skills of self-description. The narrator of the poem uses verbal tools to create her own portrait. But the painter, sculptor, and photographer also have many tools: trained eyes, skill at the rendering of fabric, construction of distance and space, use of shadows and highlights, depiction of posture, bearing, settings. The great portrait artists dug deep in their encounters with subjects to fathom and convey their complexity. The 'inner' – the mind, the soul, the personality – is materialized, made 'outer'. From their portraits we get the sense of knowing another person, crossing that divide into the mystery. As the narrator puts it (though perhaps her meaning is skeptical or satirical), her hair 'is the wire behind the light switch' – the very rendering of the hair can be something that 'turns the picture on', making the eyes alive and inhabited, so they look back and follow us.[m]

Still, given that people are so complex, and their inner selves (their 'minds', to use the narrator's term) so elusive, how can it make sense to say as I do that a person who sits for a portrait really has an essence? How is that compatible with the narrator's sense of herself as such a complicated being? The title of my book on this topic includes the word 'Persons' because I wanted to acknowledge that people are complex natural beings.[n] We are animals, creatures with physical bodies that evolved over millennia. Like other animals, we express ourselves to the world in our postures and faces. We are entities whose physical features are intricately commingled with the activities of life. Unlike most other animals, we also express ourselves in relationship to others by posing. We deliberately convey our 'inner' nature socially: we express our thoughts, emotions, deeds, interactions and ways of being by our expressions, gestures, clothing, possessions. Our visible bodies have just the sorts of features the narrator mentions: nails bitten down, rosy cheeks, feet wearing expensive red shoes. We look back at other people through our eyes, seeing in turn through theirs into who they are, discerning their feelings, the songs they would sing, their attitudes toward others. Is this person before us deliberate or delicate, sly or sensitive, funny or frivolous? Do they provoke others with their silly smirks? Facial expressions and bodily features *are* a person, and the time someone has lived adds up and inscribes upon them the record of their life – their essence – now open to reading by the sharp observer, skilled poet, and portrait artist.

— CF

Learning to Eat

Learning to eat again
is like learning to run
down a mountainside,
I mean really run, your
legs freewheeling,
your ribs bright spokes
in your chest. It's like
learning to fall asleep
in someone else's arms,
or like that exercise in art
class where you don't
look down at the page
until the end to see
the bulbous, lovely
shapes you've made.
I have acquired the
language of colour
and shade. I have
renounced the minimalism
of Ryvita and apple peel.
I have abandoned
the expressionism
of meat-rind in the plant pots
potatoes hidden in pockets
sponge pudding pushed
around the bowl. So,

when you place a dish
of mackerel down
in front of me on our first
meal together, I see
the jewelled detail
of blackberries, the sweep
of buttered mash,
the texture of kale.
I say this is a masterpiece
and mean it, then
you arrange each
artful item
on the plate
and together
we demolish it.

— HM

Mash, Mackerel, Masterpiece

This poem makes me really happy. It is remarkable to me that Helen Mort could make such a beautiful, flowing, moving leap from my earnest attempt to write about meals and artistic value.° Her poem does the thing that I love but do not understand about poetry, as it packs more into its forty-one short lines than can fit into pages and pages of a philosophical essay. Let me try to talk about what that 'more' is.

Her title is 'Learning to Eat', and the first line is 'Learning to eat again'. This is a hook for me right away, because I do not think of eating as something I learned to do or would have to relearn. But that thought has changed by the end of the poem. The first simile given to tell us about learning to eat again, that it 'is like learning to run / down a mountainside', is a great image of bodily freedom and almost tumbling downhill motion – but the mystery of the hook is still there. Why do we need to learn this? Can't we just let gravity and the mountainside have their way with us? But with that vivid motion in mind, you can remember that although it is in a way natural and hard *not* to do, it is also not exactly *easy* to do. It takes coordination and concentration and being ready to adjust at a moment's notice. The poem brings out how eating does and does not 'come naturally' to us. We will eat somehow or other, if there is food available, but we will not inevitably eat in a way that has the freedom, energy and finely adjusting, coordinating ease that can be had. We may have to learn it, and part of what the poem does is make that project bigger or deeper than I made it. I was trying to say that in having meals, though we are not constituting works of art – roughly because meals resist the pointed purpose and integrity of art – we can do things with artistic value. That value involves 'taking reflective charge' of possibilities for goodness. This poem takes charge in that way: as I am trying to say here, I could not have seen the possibilities for goodness that happen in this poem. It does this in part by making the 'masterpiece' of a meal be a matter of people meaning that it be so to each other. Maybe this is a deft, heartening argument against my claim – if so, I don't mind! In the vocabulary of the poem, that we learn to eat well, perhaps happily demolishing a dish of buttered mash and mackerel together, seems to be hard and easy. It is not only a matter of artistic value; it takes openness to what people are, as bodily, artful, moving, learning beings.

— EJ

The Tattooed Lady

'It hurt something awful, but it was worth it'.
– Betty Broadbent

Portrait of Betty at a beauty pageant, the wingspan
of her small black cape. Portrait of Betty lifting up her dress
to show her thighs. Portrait of the portrait of Pancho Villa
on her leg, Madonna almost smiling from her back.
Then Betty with a zebra at the circus, tight grip
on the fur tufting its neck. Betty naked,
wearing socks and sandals, seated,
with a crystal ball at stomach height.

Betty in another century, in miniature,
an outline on a younger woman's arm,
or Betty at the end, her hands steepled
in front of her, her horn rimmed
spectacles and level stare,
her last designs on us.

— HM

Being Betty: Tattoos and Transfiguration

In 2015, I wrote an article entitled 'Ink, Art, and Expression: Philosophical Questions about Tattoos' for *Philosophy Compass*.[P] In it, I raised questions about the ethical import of tattoos, their significance as expressions of identity, and their possible status as art. If tattoos could count as art, I wondered (and that was still an open question), would they offer some unique contribution that other works of art did not? How radical could the difference be between paint applied to canvas and ink applied to human skin? Somewhere at the tangled intersection of identity and expression and artistic impact lies a possible answer about the unique aesthetic potential of tattoos. Sometimes a tattoo – when it is extensive enough, or radical enough, or well executed enough, or compelling enough in whatever it is that it conveys – becomes something in terms of which its bearer can be seen.

So, with respect to a tattoo's art status: can a tattoo be more than just a decoration? And if tattoos can be art, might they do something further that other kinds of art do not? Might they transmute the person others see, allow their bearers to embrace the kind of otherness that gives them license to run away, join the circus, open windows into other worlds? Can we rewrite ourselves in ink?

Sometimes we display the tattoo on our arm as if it were a picture on the wall, although I want to say that this is not always all there is to our tattoos. Look here: a rose, a skull, Ruth Bader Ginsburg on my bicep. Pretty, no? Check out the realism. Love me some RBG! Very often there's nothing more than that to a tattoo. But there can be more. Just look at Betty, who inked herself into a lifelong three-ring festival. Sometimes we *are* the work, in that the work inflects the human canvas. Betty Broadbent was a *populated* woman: an entire country occupied by queens and saints and revolutionaries, glimpses of whom could be permitted or withheld. Her choice, always.

Inga Duncan Thornell became Galadriel – she was, after a bilateral mastectomy, tattooed with gorgeous vines and ferns and flowers[q]. More and more often, women choose body art over reconstructive surgery, challenging conceptions of the beautiful. Thornell's tattoos were (I admit to thinking when I saw the photographs) better than breasts, the winds of Middle Earth almost audibly rustling across her skin. 'It hurt something awful,' it is reported that Betty Broadbent said, 'but it was worth it.' Thornell felt much the same. The chest piece took one Sunday a month for two and a half years to tattoo, and more was to be added after that. Thornell is extraordinary in a way that it is difficult to describe, entwined in all that lush, ensorcelled verdure, replacing loss and dispossession with flowering and growth. You look at her and you don't see a patient, a victim, a sufferer. You don't see someone who is no longer whole. You see the lady of Lórien, the Lady of the Golden Wood.

— EMD

CODAS

Coffee, Poetry and Philosophy

It has been said that one can philosophise about anything.[r] But philosophers have largely neglected coffee. Not because they don't like it. In my experience, philosophers – lots of them at least – *really* like coffee. (If you want to find a philosopher quickly in Leeds, look for them in Opposite Cafe. If you want to know what's really going on at a philosophy conference, stand near the coffee urns.) But it can't be said that there has been a lot of philosophical work on coffee.[s]

Poetry was neglected by philosophers for a long time too, but there has been a recent uptick of philosophical interest in the topic.[t] What's going on? Might philosophy of coffee be the next big thing?

Philosophers, especially philosophers of art, are into *aboutness* in its varied guises: content, meaning, representation, and so on. Of course that's not the only thing they are into, but it is often precisely when aboutness of some form or other is involved that philosophers think there is some interesting work to be done.

The problem with coffee, then, should be pretty obvious. Where's the content? Where's the meaning? When it comes to coffee you don't usually even find the minimal forms of representation that one can find with other sorts of food. Animal crackers! Cookie Puss! Gingerbread houses! (One exception that you might have thought of is latte art.[u]) Of course, a cup of coffee might mean a lot to you first thing in the morning, but *meaning to you*, or even *meaning to me*, is not the sort of meaning that philosophers are typically that interested in.

So coffee's apparent lack of aboutness is, I suspect, one of the important reasons it has been almost entirely neglected as a topic of philosophical interest.

And what about poetry? Isn't *it* a meaningful thing – a *really meaningful thing* at that? Helen's poems surely traffic in meaning. So why was poetry largely neglected by contemporary philosophers of art until just recently?

It is not a lack of meaning or aboutness that led to poetry's neglect. But it is the case that many of the most interesting issues about poetry are not about meaning per se but, rather, about its formal features. And it is also the case that there are certain kinds of content – content that is straightforwardly and unambiguously expressible by language – that philosophers, philosophers of art in particular, seem to find easier to deal with. That kind of content is not always so central to poetry.

Poetry isn't really being neglected by philosophers now. I'm tempted to say that it's trendy. I wonder if philosophy of coffee could become trendy. On the one hand, it seems unlikely. Poetry is a central mode of human meaning making. We make sense of the world around us in terms of poems. That isn't true of coffee. But on the other hand, coffee is involved in many robustly meaningful mental states: experiences of coffee, thoughts about coffee, coffee imaginings, desires for coffee, and so on. And philosophy just isn't really limited to dealing with aboutness. There's more to the world, and to philosophy, than representation. So coffee's meaning deficit shouldn't preclude a philosophy of coffee, although I'm not sure that's enough to underwrite a philosophical trend.

Philosophy, then, can, and I think should, address both coffee and poetry. One can write philosophical poems and poems about coffee. [v] Coffee, although it can't be about poetry or philosophy (because it can't be about anything at all), fuels poets and philosophers and their conversations. Helen has shown us how a philosophical paper might inspire the creation of a poem, and her interlocutors show us various ways a poem might spur philosophical reflection. Are these the only connections between the three domains?

— AM

That Chatty, Caffeinated Feeling

Philosophers love to talk. Real philosophy gets done when we're hanging out in cafes, at the bars after the conference, espresso in hand, beer in hand, revving us up, winding us down. It might seem strange that these two opposite things work so well – the stimulant and relaxant – to juice all that thinking. The mind shifts pace. Coffee accelerates me, and it focuses me – the world narrows down and I can lose myself in the minutiae. A beer or a swig of whiskey loosens me up; I stop sweating the details and let myself skip around, sketch large frameworks, make big goofy connections.

Sometimes I think that it's not just the particular shift, but the fact of change itself. My mind moves down certain channels, and the various drugs force it into a new track. I have to think the same things through again, but with a different mind. And while I track down one idea, while taking myself through every level of caffeination and inebriation, then I have a spectrum of versions of myself, thinking from different moods and paces, about the same thing.

Conversation gets us a different version of the same thing. It gets us out of the trap of our own head. I think this is a common experience for every philosopher – and probably every academic, every writer, or, really, every thoughtful human being. You walk down the same ruts and you think you've got everything figured out, every peg in the right place, and then you start talking to somebody else and all your clarity falls to shambles, and you mourn for it… but then you suddenly start thinking new thoughts, and usually better ones.

Maybe this is why we like to do these things together. A cup of coffee with your work, a beer in the afternoon maybe – a regular life of solitary drinking is the norm for a lot of philosophers.

But the real magic is when you're getting to talk and then that hit of espresso buzz slams into your brain. It's a collision of different mental gearshifts. And if that's true for talking to other philosophers, it's doubly true when we get to talk to our opposites across the aisle – the artists, the poets. I'm used to having to expand my mind to cope with another philosopher, with their slightly different rational methodologies and theoretical presuppositions. But bouncing back and forth with a poet is a very different kind of mental motion – one where I had to remember that reasoning is just one little tiny shred of the way our minds can move.

— CTN

Notes

a   Peter Lamarque, 'Poetry and Abstract Thought.' *Midwest Studies in Philosophy*, 33 (2009): 37-52.

b   Jorge J.E. Gracia, 'Borges's "Pierre Menard": Philosophy or Literature?' *The Journal of Aesthetics and Art Criticism*, 59 (2001): 45-57.

c   Peter Kivy, 'Paraphrasing Poetry (for Profit and Pleasure).' *The Journal of Aesthetics and Art Criticism*, 69 (2011): 367–377.

d   Aaron Meskin and Jon Robson, 'Taste and Acquaintance.' *The Journal of Aesthetics and Art Criticism* 73 (2015)): 127 – 139.

e   For a discussion and overview of these issues see Jon Robson, 'Aesthetic Testimony.' *Philosophy Compass* 7 (2012): 1-10.

f   John Dyck and Matt Johnson, 'Appreciating Bad Art.' *The Journal of Value Inquiry* 51 (2017): 279-292.

g   C. Thi Nguyen, 'The Aesthetics of Rock Climbing.' *The Philosophers' Magazine* 78 (2017): 37-43.

h   Sherri Irvin, 'Scratching an Itch.' *The Journal of Aesthetics and Art Criticism*, 66 (2008): 25–35.

i   Nicholas Alden Riggle, 'Street Art: The Transfiguration of the Commonplaces.' *The Journal of Aesthetics and Art Criticism* 68 (2010): 243-57.

j   Jeanette Bicknell, 'Excess in Art: The Case of Oversinging.' *The Journal of Aesthetics and Art Criticism* 76 (2018): 83-92.

k   A.W. Eaton, 'Robust Immoralism.' *The Journal of Aesthetics and Art Criticism*, 70 (2012): 281-292.

l   A.W. Eaton, 'Where Ethics and Aesthetics Meet.' *Hypatia: A Journal of Feminist Philosophy* 18 (2003): 159–88.

m   As I argued in 'Portraits in Painting and Photography,' the portrait typically has two aims, the revelatory and the creative, which can sometimes come into conflict. See Cynthia Freeland, 'Portraits in Painting and Photography.' *Philosophical Studies* 135 (2007): 95-109.

n   Cynthia Freeland, *Portraits and Persons* (Oxford: Oxford University Press, 2010).

o   Eileen John, 'Meals, Art, and Artistic Value.' *Estetika* 51 (2014): 254-69.

p   E.M. Dadlez, 'Ink, Art and Expression: Philosophical Questions about Tattoos.' *Philosophy Compass* 10 (2015).

q   Inga Duncan Thornell, 'My Mastectomy Tattoo.' https://web.archive.org/web/20181129142819/https://dunthor.com/2012/07/31/tattoo-tuesday/. Accessed October 1, 2018.

r   See https://web.archive.org/web/20120120164004/http://schwitzsplinters.blogspot.com/2012/01/for-all-x-theres-philosophy-of-x.html.

s   But there is some. See Scott F. Parker and Michael W. Austin (eds), *Coffee: Philosophy for Everyone, Grounds for Debate* (Chichester, UK: Wiley-Blackwell, 2011). Brian Williams' *The Philosophy of Coffee* (British Library Publishing, 2018) is, in fact, a short book about the history of coffee.

t   For discussion of the neglect, see Anna Christina Ribeiro, 'Toward a Philosophy of Poetry,' *Midwest Studies in Philosophy* 33 (2009): 61-77. For recent work on the topic, see John Gibson, *The Philosophy of Poetry* (Oxford: Oxford University Press, 2015).

u   See my 'Latte Art as Art' available at the Food& website: https://web.archive.org/web/20160304071422/http://www.foodand.co.uk/latte-art-as-art/.

v   Helen's poem 'Testimony' is set in a cafe and, at least in part, is about coffee. See also Canto 3 of Pope's 'Rape of the Lock'.

Author and Editor Biographies

Helen Mort is a poet, novelist and lecturer in creative writing at the Manchester Writing School, Manchester Metropolitan University. Her work has been shortlisted for the T.S. Eliot Prize and the Costa Award. Her first novel *Black Car Burning* has just been published by Chatto & Windus, and she has also written plays, short stories and creative non-fiction. She is a Fellow of the Royal Society of Literature.

Aaron Meskin is Professor of Philosophical Aesthetics at the University of Leeds. He works on a variety of issues in philosophical aesthetics, the philosophy of food, and philosophical psychology. Aaron is the editor and author of numerous publications including *The Routledge Companion to Comics* (2016) and *The Art of Comics: A Philosophical Approach* (Wiley-Blackwell 2012). In July 2019, Aaron will begin as Head of the Department of Philosophy at the University of Georgia.

Contributor Biographies

Jeanette Bicknell is the author of *Why Music Moves Us* (Palgrave 2009) and *Philosophy of Song and Singing: An Introduction* (Routledge 2015). She works as a professional mediator in Toronto, Canada.

E.M. Dadlez is a professor of philosophy at the University of Central Oklahoma, writing on issues at the intersection (often at the collision) of aesthetics, ethics and epistemology. She has written two books on the preceding, in addition to editing a collection entitled *Jane Austen's Emma: Philosophical Perspectives* for Oxford University Press.

John Dyck is a PhD candidate in philosophy at the CUNY Graduate Center in New York City, where he is finishing a dissertation on aesthetic value. John is still trying to figure out how so much truly awful stuff can be so, so good. He also writes on philosophy of music, increasingly on country music.

A.W. Eaton is an associate professor in the philosophy department at the University of Illinois-Chicago. She writes about painting, the relationship between ethics and aesthetics, and various topics in feminism.

Cynthia Freeland is Professor Emerita of Philosophy at the University of Houston and past president of the American Society for Aesthetics. She has published on topics in ancient philosophy, feminist philosophy, film theory, and aesthetics. Her books include *But Is It Art?* (Oxford 2001) and *Portraits and Persons* (Oxford 2010).

Sherri Irvin is a professor and administrator at the University of Oklahoma. She has been known to write quirky philosophy articles and create mediocre pottery.

Eileen John is a Reader in Philosophy at the University of Warwick. Her research is in aesthetics and philosophy of literature. She is especially interested in the cognitive and ethical significance of art. She is currently Co-Director of the Centre for Research in Philosophy, Literature and the Arts at Warwick.

C. Thi Nguyen is associate professor of philosophy at Utah Valley University. He used to be a food writer; now he's a rock climber. His book, *Games: Agency as Art*, is forthcoming from Oxford University Press.

Nick Riggle teaches philosophy at the University of San Diego. His work focuses on areas where the line between art and life is blurred: personal style, ideals, invitations, beauty's transformative power, social art, and street art, among other things. His recent book *On Being Awesome* (Penguin 2017) is a popular treatment of many of these themes.

Jon Robson is Assistant Professor of Philosophy at The University of Nottingham. He is co-editor of *Aesthetics and the Sciences of Mind* (OUP 2014) and *The Aesthetics of Videogames* (Routledge 2018) and co-author of *A Critical Introduction to the Metaphysics of Time* (Bloomsbury 2016).

Acknowledgements

'The Tattooed Lady' first appeared in *The Poetry Review*.

Thanks to Douglas Caster and The University of Leeds for a Douglas Caster Cultural Fellowship which made this publication possible. Thanks also to Jamie McGarry at Valley Press and to all the contributors.